DATE DUE

W9-CLN-893

Kyotologic

ANNE GORRICK

Kyotologic

—The Pillow Book Poems—

Shearsman Books
Exeter

Published in the United Kingdom in 2008 by
Shearsman Books Ltd
58 Velwell Road
Exeter EX4 4LD

ISBN 978-1-84861-004-0

Acknowledgments
Some of these poems have appeared in the following journals: *American Letters and Commentary, Cipher Journal, Dislocate, Fence, Fish Drum, Good Foot, Gutcult, Hunger, No Tell Motel, Seneca Review,* and *Sugar Mule.*

The poem '171. Illnesses' was anthologized in *The Bedside Guide to No Tell Motel* (No Tell Books, 2006).

It is with gratitude to Tony Frazer at Shearsman Books that this book now lives in the world on paper instead of solely in the air.

Thank you for your encouragement over many art and writing-filled years: Janis Benincasa, Steve Cotten, Teresa Genovese, Kathleen Gilligan, Maria Gorrick, and Art and Marcella Levin.

10,000 thanks to Peter Genovese without whom this work would have no shelter, and to Maryrose Larkin without whom this book would not exist.

Additional appreciation to the Catskill Center and their generous encouragement in the form of their artist-in-residence program, which lent some time and space to do this work. Inverna Lockpez's belief in artistic risk-taking has been both a roadsign and a relief.

CONTENTS

Notes:

"Otology – the science of the ear and its diseases." One possible definition of poetry . . .

Written at the turn of the second millennium, these poems are a rethinking, a modernization of sections from *The Pillow Book of Sei Shonagon* which was written at the end of the first millennium by a Japanese courtesan during the Heian period. I began with the Ivan Morris translation.

2. Especially Delightful is the First Day

Lucky	Blue horses in borrowed arcs
	escorted by laughter
	A certain number of injuries make up the
	slats of a fence
thoughts	as though they lived all their lives
	Considering the vastness and texture of their faces
	Unpleasant as the sun brought back
nine	into a garden of melting snow
	The horses in procession extravagantly
times	and she narrows into her carriage

Her grasp separated her from her house
supervision, division
Blue horses laugh outside the offices of reason
She walked like a fortunate thought, vastness
Here the skin of the land sunk simultaneously as a garden
where snow dissolves

The	Remembered opportunity
	borrowed to form protections
end of	They traveled turning lucky thoughts into a woman
	The country's vastness runs past the moving car
	The surface quality as propellant
injury	When skin became the country of the garden

Ring in eight dreamt surroundings
What kinds of injuries are sustainable?
When the fortune of women has some good pebbles in it
The immense countries of thought, protections
Her eyes are unpleasant simultaneously
That place where her skin sank and became another country
Disjointed, melted, visible: she
The method we happen inside the car
in a queue of luxury

	In a remembered field
dreamt	the palace of the blue horse
	Several senior flatteries the color of a house
	The curve of an escort
	They prance when laughter stops making the horse blue
surroundings	the color of twanging

Look at the way the door is placed in the wall
She dims about the garden
in a predetermined amount
The enormous lands of an argued palace
To be able to look at the texture of facts
Each place and its skin
its demonstrated awkward
dark patch where the snow begins to melt
The sense in occurrence

	Blue palaces in a remembered field
Rub	Blue palaces in a remembered field
	Compliments about houses
it	Horses: when their color is dependent on laughter
	or prance and twanging
	The palace walls dim, depending on method
with	Fortunate thoughts inspect a woman
	blown apart appropriately
	In order to dissolve a patch of land
snow	rub it with snow

What exactly does this field think it was?
The end of color?
They try to stop the curve of a watch
Because of laughter and produced fact
It will hop and it will come and go
and it will ask and the thing will do
and it will ring

	The double meaning of a house
color	The prosecuting attorney and the thought of a woman

where the fortune is good, order approximate
The possibility inside walking
ends   An immediacy that reports surface quality
To burn a piece of cloth in order to make it visible

Stop short of the fact that the horse
when their colors are blue, laughter is made
caracolent in resound
Snails, winding staircases
We are reliable about injury to the garden
A lucky idea woman inspects me
blown in her components
You have demonstrated him in order to dissolve

Caracolent   Ground that should begin in snow
          His gardens of skin are difficult to handle in the dark
in   Reliable in the injury garden
          When the color blue is the result of laughter
          In skin gardens: the snow, a difficult darkness
resound   What have we underlined here?

In high degrees of enterprise
the horse a blue color, am
Notice the fact which forms itself from the color blue
To debate the enormous actually surrounds
but it did not burn in components
When place dissolves from soil
In the skin garden, snow driven: a supposed place

          The delays in tablecloths
          Hop and will come and will be gone
unscrolled   and ask also of the thing
          The foreheads of deer in offices
          After territory: thin places
          The woman at a method significance
in   unscrolled in quatrains
          This place is protected by possibility

or in a palace of last dependences
Refute the clock

quatrains   Regular skins in place of soil

3. On the Third Day of the Third Month

Luminous   Willows charm the season
                 When a visitor is posed close to conversation
calms   When the peach blossoms enter the sky
                 as he is disseminated beneath leaves
in   Once blossoms scatter
                 a huge pleasure ends in a vase
                 Possible his majesty
sun   Any situation inspired prettily by wings

When the shining sun calms down
and the peach trees take over
The pastures are enclosed
in continuous screws, always, in silk
The willow too is enchantingly seasonal
After extended sheets of rain, she finds him without attraction
All trees actually lose their charm once
in their large pleasure of stopping
Next to the long address of the cherry tree
a usual guest or one of their sovereignties
The visitor carries a coat made from cherry skins

He   I am one that likes the fact that the March day
                 is written brightly by a spring sky
is   An illumination and calm: the sun
                 Wood excessively cocooned in silkworms
seasonal   After leaves spread, as for me, there is no harm
                 Actually when the flowers start to disperse
in   everything wooden loses its charm
                 The vase rearranged into a larger joy
his   Spoken vicinities, visitors installed, how pleasant
                 Altitude: the usual guest of the Empress
                 or perhaps 1 o'clock
joy   Cherry appears bottom to the body in all cases

It is the third day of the third month
she tastes the shine of the calm sun
The willow charms us out of our stations
The buds enclosed as the
without-ends of silk and its occasions
In fact, trees lose their enchantment with time
An office of cherry trees, a great pleasure to break
and arrange in a great vase
A seated colloquy
In all cases the visitor will wear a colorful coat
made from carefully cut cherries
Out from under this vestment she emerges

The   The third month is drawn with a good pen inside the sky
             and the sun shines at a constant temperature
             The spectacle peels from later
spectacle   and the peach tree blooms in the form of hours
             The willow in bud besieges a seasonalness
             As the leaves spread outside against fact
peels   the blossoms sprinkle lost charm as soon as actually

Months are drawn inside spring
the play taken off it for now
Nevertheless together within its cocoon
charm is a season, a point of reference
Fact lost in blossomed spray
All trees lose their charm as soon as it all is really begun
He arranges pleasure in a large vase
Over distance virtue expires in possibility
Face to face, he is even I, and we are luckier

not   A third outgoing, motivating force dawns
             inside the sky and the sun constantly polishes her
hardly   The silkworm besieged with fascination
             Any reference ages them
             Sheets scatter, that all trees lose their fascination
really   The graceful virtue of distances

The sky and "whatever" is the temperature of that relationship
Night opens inside the fixed and glossy sun
You say "all wooden fascination is really almost not lost"
but in fact, stars in their beautiful method closings
Possible the visitors who spare that which you do not know
The colors inside this type
Fact remakes you out of time's random and elegant intervals

A	The solar luster, force and motive
	March 3rd, and the sky of what temperature
	Hour and hour: silk besieged in remainder
visible	The tree almost loses its cocooned fascination
	a comfortable reference to age and insect
That	How we scatter the facts with begin
	Joy organized in beautiful method, a mastered place
	From the magnetic pole, a cherried soprano
in	carried the box from master attachment
	He connects uniformly with writing
	against hazard hours
fascination	He will make fact possible in elegant intervals

The payment of night to the sun
Gloss and force that give reason to a 3 sky-ed March
The joy in beautiful closings peeled
Sisters are sufficient to fact
a pocket of virtue, one hour of risk
Almost intervaled, an elegant fate

where	The payment of night in leaves glossed reason
	absent-minded in regard to the scatter of fascination
	where the She actually begins
the	In place of color, the thing of it all in sheets of rain
	Butterflies: paperbags of virtue in a dangerous hour
She	Distance forms possibility, which is an elegant fate

In place of the absent-minded you, relative to scatter
The letter shuts sufficiently
The Him is actual, distantly formed

A	In compensation for the leaves that fall at night
	The flower of this axis nevertheless comes
translation	Then hour and hour: the silk
	besieges the rest in comfort and charm
by	in insect obvious
	The cherry blossoms disseminate joy
	organized in beautiful fallen enclosures
force	A lucky form of you in dangerous in hours

The sky marches in threes
Time is insect obvious
In the distracted place, she elongatedly sews
a dress made from bruised cherries
Possibility associates with him in elegance

Besieged	The compensation of leaves for night interprets reason
	Three skies in March, sipped temperature along its axis
in	Hour and hour, the silk!
	In place of abstraction, dissemination
comfort	loss elongatedly

Cherry trees along an empire's reservoir
enterprise and joy
A flower placed under restrictions
organized in beautiful enclosures
A river exemption, she is arranged all over the place
in boxes of proportion and color nevertheless
This lucky you, a bag of virtue
in one hour's worth of danger
This is real time and distance, informed possibility
an elegant fate

A	The remuneration of leaves
	at night, solarinterned
	The luster and force of his reasons
	The sky marches away from us and the temperature dips
place	If the flower, then nevertheless

then hour and hour, that silk!
Information surrounds us now internally
This time, its insect obvious
She connects outside to outside
distracted   When fascination disperses

She and she elongatedly says
"The broken axis along a bruised cherry"
Water to unload the river
organized in closings, more beautiful than method
It assumes, the Great Emergency, held nearby
The color of the thing covers the inner with the inner
the subject of her magnetic soprano
In place of proportion, He takes cut laws out of a box
He sufficiently closes the letter to a lucky person
One hour of danger seen
his distances informed by a cherried elegance

4. How Delightful Everything Is

Thus   How delicious us all per hour
     The sheets, which do not always cover the trees too
     abundantly
     are green and fresh
     No fog to hide to the sky or throw a glance upward
     we are surmounted by beauty
disappears One evening slightly cloudy, or the night
     thus disappears doubt in one's own ears
     Men loosely wrapped in purple paper, long boxes
     The nuanced unequaled by borders
     Dying seems more attractive than usual
     Girls in daily clothing, disordered
doubt   separated at the seams

Barely, in the evening, become cloudy
Night for a second time
Night doubts you faintly
Loose paper in a long box:
green applied to yellow
This time or year borders on shadow
dyeing everything with normality
Girls are young in their everydays
a large confusion of clothing
wrinkled connections, broken

in   You by beautiful overcome
     Evening swindled of clouds
     The holiday is loose on me
     yellow wrapped suitably
     Color: a material pleasure in root purple
     The border shadows rolled up, dyes all
greatly   The young in their daily formations
     As for the girl occasionally
     in greatly chaotic clothing
chaotic   possibility wrinkles, breaks

How pleasant is work as holiday?
Day overcome by fog
in the time of the interval-bird's song
Yellow wrapped in green paper
Color as matter, the pleasure in question
The holiday celebrates me loosely
This year, time bordered in shadow
Attraction, comparison dyes the ground around the girl

in	Too still wooden become green
	Search procedures for the sky in fog
interval	You: an announcement from an interval of birds
	Yellow and green rolled up in a long box
of	deeply, deeply waving
	The colors of an affair, pleasure
birds	a chaotic break, when the girl becomes a prayer to him

Isn't it too much to come out of green
his heart strong and paid for?
The sky masked in fog, surpluses so splendid and concerned
The night related to me, deceived
A second form of like in time
The box is a long holiday in yellow and green rolled
to celebrate you out of reach
undulating in achievement, deeply, deeply
As for joy in the color business
the question of how you see yourself this year
time rolled entirely in charm
A level of comparison and nuanced edges
Chaotic clothing connects the daily side of arrangement
As for that ardently disordered possibility
many somethings relative to clothing
The everyday side of rearrangement related to her

This	The day is a holiday from banking
	silent in the center of green
first	Everyday is granted by the sky

	Research, surplus, gorgeous
and	It is like this first and that
	An amended song and the bird selecting it
	Place moves about weakly, a hazard in method
that	Inside the hour, belief is firmly the candle that deceives

Loose and placed in a box of because
in long holiday green rolls
This article waves frantically in yellow
celebrates deeply deeply to peel
You are outside all my questions
Intelligence not measured in hours
a whole leveling instrument
The writing is passionate, mascara-ed
regards a possibility disordered to many silences
The everyday side of this mouth's clothing
a thin temporary damage

	Not a strong center of green
That	Daily sky, masked and mist
	excessively gorgeous
cover	The night diluted by its hours
	Candles delude you
	A box filled with insideout holidays
	commemorate the end of our arrival
the	His edges are masked with intelligence
	his whole numbers enchanted
	Clothes that cover the mouth
mouth	damages being provisory

Today is a model holiday from banking
Quiet directions, centered green
Granted daily, the sky masks process and research
with a gorgeous excess
Regarding the notification, one amends one's height to it
Danger being equal moves toward weakness
The hours diluted in candlelight

and a long green box filled with holidays
Joy in the method of color
A masked edge, this intelligence that is not an hour:
whole numbers, enchantment, instrument, comparison
The writing is passionately disordered
by a lump of many silences
Enthusiasm clothes her mouth

as if   One grants to him a daily sky, masked in fog
               the process of research
               a splendid excess: the wind
he   She is amorphous, a long green box
               filled with bearings and holidays
               This back and forth of yellow, as if he was an article
was   an almost vague extension, deeply deeply to peel
               The end of arrival
an   The intelligence in hours and whole numbers
               A magic spell rolled up the comparisons of years and colors
               Where nuance is silent enthusiasms
article   culture pays with our mouths

We reached the point where strong green is accomplished
an everyday mask of fog
undeserved forms, intervals
The morning types its methods into him
The night misunderstands him, thins
A movement of skin commemorated deeply deeply
by a long green box
The green place of yellow in a holiday
There are times when you mask an edge with intelligence
and paint around it
He: a magical spelling, an appliance
a nuanced integer: this year
Writing on the everyday side of place
where disorder is damaged
culture is provisory, apart

air   Days exit in a model of interruptions
      Explicit elements in a process called "research"
is   march across a sky masked in fog
      The locomotion of the skin, solid and extended
      an amorphous memory deep deep
undeserved This yellow place green, an article bearing interruptions

Because our end replaces you
years exist that mask intelligence
Magical spellings, appliances, comparison, nuanced years
Writing in restriction, union
our enthusiasms toward silence
This girl the daily side of place, disturbed by the clothing
moving inside her mouth
the destruction of her provisional culture

Clarity   There are days, all holidays, quietly good, like love
      When you reach a point that a strong green is executed
and   Motion the skin because a solid body did lengthen
      out of amorphousness and palaces
daily   commemorated deeply deeply

Holidays are indistinct roads
The appearance of order in yellow and green
You have been substituted by your edges
There will be times when magical spellings
will be connected to the enthusiasms for silence
Girls disordered by the clothes that come out of their mouths
their damaged culture provisory

16. THINGS THAT MAKE ONE'S HEART BEAT FASTER

Play	To pass a place where babies sleep in a room where incest flares
	Note their elegant Chinese even if not seen
in	Always to produce someone else's interior pleasure
Chinese	Extend in elegant Chinese, to consider become cloudy
	Smell their evening gowns, washed hair
	even if not, an inside sees
Gate	Sparrows dissipate their young
made	visit a gentleman for arrest
night	even if an inner part does not see
Mirror	Paradise wastes its people
	extended relative elegant the Chinese mirror
and	To consider time he has become cloudy
	a gentleman for the automobile
	apprehension before the relative gate
	Hats washed, scented
not it	with the nightdress on exactly
	Exactly if that one has broken does not see
	Product of these blood tapes only
	always an internal pleasure
Cloudy	The night is previous
	one without acknowledgment startled
over	The children play in sleep spaces
	A Chinese mirror to consider time
A	The night is preceding inspections of him
	To consider time for visit cloudy
	for torn a necessity
	Impregnate to inform

Visit	Because she is a form of propaganda
this	For wash-scented night, wrap function
and	Accurately, if this is the internal one
wash	was always broken not to come
	Not these adhesive tapes, an internal pleasure
it	Night proceeds beyond recognition

17. Things that Arouse a Fond Memory of the Past

The   The dried hollyhock as calligraphy
                 To find a piece of deep colored material pressed by the rain
last   It is one day rainy, and one is reamed feeling
                 and then one finds the letters from a man used to love
                 To spend time, begin to observe paper

                 A hollyhock message
                 in a piece of deep violet
night's   It is rainy and one is extended feeling
                 in order to spend time
                 and then one finds the character of a man
materials   coincidentally a man one used to love

under   To find a deep viola has colored the materials
                 She used an arrow as a message
                 On a rainy day, there is extensive sensibility to spend time
hollyhock   sensitivity broadly an end
                 One begins to observe the papers in some old way
                 And then a man finds the coincidence of characters
her   finds that he is used for love

                 Wine of the dry Rhône—a message used for her sensibility
a   Arrow headstock—a part deep viola
                 positioning grapes in order to find color
                 One day rainy and a sensitivity wide open to spend time

printed   to observe paper in some old trees
                 E then a man finds in coincidence the characters
moon   the type of coincidence that is used as excuse for love

                 When night is held up by the pages of a book

24. It Is So Stifling Hot

Very	He is gated to evening
good	The moon notes our enjoyment
	I nearly do not need to say what
to be	this consummation looks like
	Looking is spread on the floor
in	a bright new straw mat that polishes
together	insignificantly invested in the room

There was one woman left in that broken day, in the bed, in her
Lover his after
She is quilted in darkness, her head a violet decision
like the lining in a long gown
A woman who looks like rest: stiff silk, dark red, untied
How long her hair to possibly imagine

in	In the Seventh month
a	when the doors of night are kept open
frozen	Dawn and the pale ribbon of a moon, a luminous plait
	of straw
	An evening gown the color of a frozen outdoors
color	the color of a woman sunk into crimson

All the doors are held open
Measure the volume in one slat of the moon
A woman in bed took a vacation you'd love
She is absorbed into an orange dress
a sunken high red, rigid silk
its cords seem to hang as if they were left to solve the gown itself
Strong lichens in cascade introduce themselves
Her hair longs to be itself, in free fall

The	The lattices of July open, a month that awakens to time
	I, when there is no month even, enjoy that
dark	The dawn wakes as a sliver of a month

	I almost do not have the necessity or perfection of how
	to say this
magenta	The bright new straw mat where I laid it
	exactly on the part of the floor that is well liked
	The dawn has met in bed with the woman
	Gloss as, you attach a hard silk to the kind of woman
	who sleeps
is	to be solved
	His codes catch loosely at her side, the dark magenta
	of morning's body
solved	Her own hair rethinks her

The type of hours that wake us up in July
An entire month of skies thin
In order to see a splitting
you will go out to the place, and you will sleep
and you wipe yourself from falling inside
In the new straw mat, you see how fact likes the polished floor
An early aspect of hazard in the room
The permissions in women, innumerable difficulties
delay the capture of dawn
The luster and sleep solved in orange
Thick and empty
autumn name trades in place of her hair

A	He will leave and sleep will clean her
month	He is accuracy spread out before you
of	Exchange wheat for the dawn
skies	and see how much fact likes you then
end	Regard where you sleep in that hard silk place
	just the magenta side of darkness
in her	The commerce in her autumns

When consideration is a type of daylight
a divine signal looking for cracks in us
Your he will stay behind only as a form of place
the You he sleeps with and cleans

He will be accurate and disseminate you
You will think that love only occurs in daybreak
the dangerous disturbance in his song
First hunger, later fact
A code nearby, its darkness carmine softly seized the body
A name left inside of her hair

A	Because the signal of God illuminates order
	and the sky is a month's worth of conclusions
name	Cracks in their glances become speech
	Because you are new in the way you see fact, dawn
left	Sleep concerns the retention of place
	As for him, the body captured in a gown
	a scarlet vicinity, darkness grasps them quietly
behind	Place falls in tresses making that "it" possible

This maintenance and all regard bitten into this place
when the night is hot and inspected like a problem in July
The shedding of blood is quite uniform
Speech ends in cloth chapters
the cracks illuminate the shape of his mind
Out of purity and grudge you sleep
the human race sorry under accuracy
Your he: a straw mat placed on the polished floor
You peel from several dawns, trivial rooms
Finally, daybreak will be able to perform as though you were a woman
Countless permissions and the bed is difficult
Affection, aromatic, dark violet
You retain a sleep on you in orange, high and decided
My problem is with the hours found in possibility
Regard the will above writing as it falls from her sides

Slit	Maintenance, concern bite into the place where the night is hot
	Announcement illuminates
in	Substitute conclusions for months pasted to the sky
	In place of their words, fabric chapters

the   and a slit in the shape of a word
                  You sleep inside resentment and purity
shape   The You that peels because of you
                  The problem of attachment
of   depends initially on an advance into dangerous rooms

A song thinks back on its own disturbances
in unimportant rooms
Innumerable permissions, and reading is difficult
Affections, aromatic trees affect the meaning of words
The color of sleep, the color of loss
attached to a hard silk, high and undecided
The width of writing, its thickness
a name that trades in the autumn of her braids
She shook from her hair: his name

Because   Replace two pieces of an hour with suffocation
                  the summary of months without a sky
                  In place of certain words, how a fabric chapter ends in slits
of   The human races asleep under the accuracy of time
                  Corn, its straw, because of the place
this   The accomplishments of women and collecting
                  Text read with innumerable permissions
                  our inclinations to mean: a new gloss
place   Her autumns beneath the lichens of this place

We suffocate under examination
when the hours put on their boots in order to catch fire
Blood loss from the evening as dawn, evenly
Walls are compulsory indoors
an attempt to conclude months, to end the sky
Place sentences into cloth chapters
The sleep we construct in resentments and purity:
our straw limits
The you that descends because of you
Study the outlines of our method songs
The rooms are made enormous when they are locked up with women

The color of sleep, the color of loss
A woman the color of that silk attached to difficulty and is solved
A body the size of an hour, fussy about food
The will above writing, sufficient thicknesses
Autumn braids itself into place

	July will inspect your questions until you suffocate
braided	Conclusions: a cotton chapter, blood loss, her internal months
	Resentment is pure
into	You do with sleep what you want: straw pleated to its limits, for example
	Seated on this country's edge, we advance to a dangerous room
another	invested in our method songs
	Opposition a ratio more enormous than place

Locked into innumerable permissions
go and assemble a woman, a fragrant axis
her dark eyes purple, participles yawn around her
The protections in orange, sleep the color of a woman's blood loss
the difficult places are solved
The body, its food
travel in a lump of darkness: the automobile
Writing as far as possible nearby
Place braided to autumn, a falling reduction of possibility

When	Walls tighten around our internal months when the conclusion of the sky is mandatory
difficulty	Cotton chapters end, torn from form the place and the route into you
	Hostility and accuracy purify our sleep
looks	Higher numbers advance into the room with questions
	In order to satisfy the axis where fragrance is similar to her
	A new lip gloss, the color of loss
like	A woman the color of rough silk
	The body depends on a concern for food

corded to the darknesses underneath her skirt
Whether problems request my time in writing

fact   Writing, representation: a possible address
The autumns that are braided into her hair

25. FLOWERING TREES

A factory of dark sheeted plum blossoms
does not deserve special praise
Small white houses
Thin white evening gowns under a layer of greenish yellow
The poetrys that bind them to a grove of orange trees
thin and worn

Picture	Cherry, slender and branch
	Big petals and dark red leaves: how exquisite
	A finely used color
	A one-way holiday
magnificent	in faint yellow green dresses
	A four month long ending, and five beginnings
	A quilt of brilliant waste
sight	If you are foot lucky, look at the fruit
	The Japanese cherry prevents the morning rain
sight	The orange trees are well written

An I who is filled up
When the feeling of the year is good
I like the fact that you are coolly hidden
A gown that wears like refusal
attached to the body
thin, are long white and almost visible
Leaf green depths

and	April wears a shifting wastefulness
belief	When the rain is shaken from the dawn
	The weeping cherry prevents a standpoint like you
is	But I need the important agreement which we do not have
charm	Many poems written concerning concern

The plum opens darkly
because luck is fulfilled particularly in red

The plum flower and the I color in the morning
Sheets of large flowers near her address
The dark red sheet was attached to a thinning I
I like the fact that you possibly hide yourselves
cooling to that think

the   Holiday exceeded only by direction
              The dress carried like waste, yellowish green also like it
              attached to the body, long white thin
              which is the visible he
rope   She shakes out the dawn
              Luck of the fruit in this first volatile view
              evenly regards this gold yellow range of sight
and   The eastern cherry prevents our points of view
              But she needs the important agreement
              which he does not have
flower   Many poems were written and attached to orange trees

The address of a flower market
The color of a yellow nine
Place holiday and charm into a set of blue eyes
She will begin in rain at the front of the world
all respect shaken from her
You stare into like

a   Because chance is completed
              In plum light, the written you is darkly expert
green   filling the morning
              The cherry color of big market flowers
form of   Interrupted from their own charm
              the blue eyes and the wisteria are suddenly white
time   In this, their body, connected like a dress on the skin

Their wonder is long lasting, an enwrapment
Rain begins on the forehead of the world
shaken of all respect and fascination
The obligation of chance found in fruit

the rope and the flowering of morning
a golden yellow spectacle: the field
Painting and the Eastern opinion of cherry trees
But this I am important
I am not this: a contract with need
No higher degrees are attached to the poems nailed
to these orange trees, written splendidly

are   Interruptions from fascination
       excess taken
importance from the orange surface of a dream

Because possibility is finished
the plum light writes you into darkness
It is ten with the thing
The connoisseur who is also the I
The market where the eastern part is dark red

The   The address when you purchase yellow flowers in nines
       An interruption of one enchantment
world   The dress also likes green and time into yellow
       The uses of enwrapment
agitated into The cherry part that deters spectacle
       This I who importantly is not I
respect   this contract, this necessity

Possibility finished and discharged with light
Written above you is darkly expert
The I which is morning is filled above
Cherries in a large market flower with your address
The interruption of places
an enchantment in blue eyes
When dresses love the color green
and the yellow of time
Wastefulness brings this whiteness

Eating	The obligation of possibility found in fruits and vegetables
	Temporary opinion: the rope and the dawn equal to this golden spectacle
fascinates	The field, a picture, and Eastern opinion
	The gross part of cherries deter spectacle
	The shaft of the poem is orange, just this side of splendid

Because all possibility is complete
plum light writes a darkness in him
a petaled dark red appraisal
Cherry that I, giant market blossoms
He purchases nine yellows
inferior in use to her address
A year in each direction, possibly you will renovate the I

its	Place severed from magic
	an interior sees white inside a bluewhite poplar
	In its body, it takes, like, the green
	Yellow the time and wasting in formal clothes
	To know enwrapment lastingly
fruit	will rob April of its initial dream
	In orange starts, rain agitates the world
	charm and consideration
	The golden decadence that prevents painting
	A peach tree outstanding, this urgently liked and looked
	But in this I am not important
voluntary	My I is not

Written in dark actions, a 10 year old earth laid against morning
blooming with problems, in dark red appraisal
The Chinese of most remarkable Chinese
In life, the problem of time and thought
horizontal communications
exceed the white of a poplar
Perhaps it is unusual, the acquisition to connect
green yellows, a subject for wastefulness
and the use of enwrapment

Type	Constantly the rain dreams itself
	The world swings on a certain amount of place
being	This secondary gold dwindles an image
	prevents the clean sketch in a range of yellow
seen	This I is necessity in this contract
	not the I important
urgently	in the wood of many gorgeous poems

26. Festivals

Soon	Smell that enchantingly mixed: iris and sage
	All this never occurs in other situations
stays	The days empty into holiday, cloudy
	Unfinished silk wraps a simple box
behind	Whenever people need to string together

Wise brush and iris mixed with charm
The end of nine times
at the bottom of small houses filled with common people
Chrysanthemums wrapped in raw silk
so that in the end, nothing is left

Nothing	There is no at all
	People in place of a roof knitted of many colors
is	Spheres on the grass, straw raincoats, an empress
	Mums wrapped in a clear box
left	catch September directly

Ever since the 9th, the days have traded
themselves for grass
A string around anytime
pulled apart from a sphere and a sea urchin
Grass separates from her tears

In place	Time connects May to congratulations and banking
	Luxury decorates the household, and we are composed
	of want
of	The ingredient of each chance
	on the whole it is compulsion, clarity
a	The sky hums and goes inside the actual one
	The congratulation inside continuous banking
person:	A series of wheat straw raincoats
	threaded with grass the color of concrete
the roof	A sea urchin separated from grass and tears

If the window screen, then the smell of burning brush
that is of this place, an intelligent mixture of charm
Resembling everything, he is attached to banking
In place of the number 9, boats and containment
The sky hums and becomes intermittent
In the funeral country of cloth, we detach
That the silk, which is not, freely
Concreteness and the grass forms a family
Grass and she tears up violently

Grass	Common people luxuriantly embellish it out of him
and	The sky is interrupted by congratulations
	The obligations divide, promoted out of concreteness
she	A foreign boy separated from grass and tears

When the iris smells like brush on fire mixed with charm
The equivalences known as the years
Authorization, rooftops, the components of probability
Coercion is implicit, the sky hums with continuous banking
A line of raincoats made of straw
The wheat was densely woven into grass
Buckrams in the funeral country regard September
a silk that is explicit
Sea urchins separated from their grasses

A silk	The iris sags with fascination
	In place of the person: a form of permission
that is	Cloth from the country of funerals, unclear in the silk
explicit	She is when it tightens, a long rest constructed of necessity

Enchantment mixes wiseness with iris
The boat with nine walls, luxury decorates his desire
The ingredients of each possibility
a compulsion that is opening

| I | When the sky becomes a form of reading |
| | A series of raincoats: the straw: |

can	a wheat knitted puncture
	The colors do not join the country in funeral cloth
smell	This place apprehends September
	When the silk remains unopened
	Is the person, then the rope, always?
it	She distributes obligation
	simulated in concrete and sea urchin

Place mixed with enchantment
In place of a person: her permission
A roof made of iris
luxuriantly decorated with marriage
Ingredient or possibility differently
Circumstance does not occur as compulsion
A geometric model in four skies
the hum of it changed the interior

What	Raincoats: straw or wheat?
	The curtains in an internally amiable palace
we	The color of concrete: the funeral cloth
	September immediately
all	where the day is changed with possibility
want	Obligation is distributed in him

When the iris and I smell this place
an unwise mixture in the brush
All competitions not connected to May end in congratulations
In place of an almost new person: the iris
The sky sighs and I read its humming sound
Raincoats crowded and woven in wheat straw
She distributes the sea urchin's concrete separation into sea and tears

The	All competitions end in magic
	whether the iris or me
problem	You attach the roof for an almost new person
	A washbasin is the center of permission
of	Inhabitant, decoration, luxuriantly
possibility	Raw materials not happening, the inferior remains of power

In order to change our internal celebrations, change the sky
Straw congested, knitted in two stabs
The physical funeral thing in cotton
You grasp with capture inside September
Silk should open the season's possibility
The box of the place
Is the person when the rope, always?

ocean   Time lingers, a mixture of lake and iris
                The iris supervises the roof
and   Congratulations indicate a hazard in the sky
                Silk from seasonal
urchin   peel the concrete from separation

Time lacquers each iris
a roof made of human hands
Interior truths of a sky at risk
The noise finishes him
Cornstraw, his I is interior
The silk of seasonal possibility
Why do families celebrate banking?
Necessity makes time a cord to anybody, any place
The concrete separation of ocean from urchin

27. TREES

A Japanese maple's dark red glare
Bloodgood sheeted outside a green environment
I will not say absolutely anything
A white pine crowned with festivals
The tree as divine presence
muddled branches, alarmingly
mathematically divided into a thousand like love
At night he imitates the noise of rain on her skin

To	Dark red leaves, a profound impression of green
lose	A parasitic biology sets up an imperial scared dance
	Her regard for the gods of existence
blossoming	The branches of the camphor frighten her
	estrange her from regard
	Because the tree is divided into 1,000 branches
Because	it describes a woman in love

A dark red book and a willow, an orange tree
Emperors and saints dance between the pine needles
The holidays imply the gods as existent
The camphor's grace grows implicitly
Rain gives a correct and pleasant imitation of itself

Chinese	The orange wood, five-needled
	Red darkly from the green of a thing
	opened deeply into another shining wood
Chinese	The gods adjusted themselves above her
	into a parasitic biology
	She can taste the dance of the holy empire
	Thought always exists as the gods of existence
hawthorn	But "palaces protracting along three edges . . ."
	May rains give an imitation of goodness

When the green of the thing into deep red darkness: the tree
Biology is parasitic
New stars are about an hour long, from end to end
the length of the dance of an empire
The holiday tastes of nothing when it's gone
Favor camphor in order for a thousand trees to call one person "in love"
The silence peels away any troublesome song
The rain imitates his good sense

She	Pine, box elder, orange timber
	She is huge with numbers, luminous
	Thinking of trees, a form of god's existence
the	The feeling of being very good: all the timber in the world
	When entanglement, estrangement become astonishment
	What tree branches call love
hour	the rain gives a sentiment of goodness

She will be used alongside pine
during the dance of an empire
Used and pine, maple and orange wood five needled
The dark red is engaged deeply, a bright lost to the woods
Digital, relative, spindle
He thinks the gods always exist in the achievement of existence
The feeling is extremely good, there is peace in the woods
even the camphor is benevolent
Relative that tangle, the I becomes estranged
1,000 branches describe her as if by telephone

(not)	Large, numerical, relative
	she becomes fact, a perfection expressed in parasite
for	All good avoids you, he thinks
	1,000 bridal branches divided into love, into cedar
delight	Healthy in the rain, the finer feelings of imitation

If the red pine, then the orange wood, five needled
A red from the green of the thing
opened deeply

Dark leaves, a bright impression
She is forced to express a parasitic biology
In her, the empire dances like time or a dress
As for the gods of existence, their thoughts are of trees
There is a point: good very, but what it is? Felt
Avoid camphor, her eyes never lift

Luminous   The estrangement of the I from the unexpected
              In meaning, what the woods call "love"
              is really 10,000 naked people in a photograph
              Branches of Himalayan cedar: a thought palace assembled
              Like orange annoyed by wood
              He is red from the green of the thing
lost   a dark sheet over the forest, and occasionally a bright
                  impression
              The holy dance of the realm,
              She likes holidays that look like you
beyond   Always this concerns the gods of existence
              their thoughts of trees point out how belief is quite good
love   She is their address, an imitation of their goodness

43. Poetic Subjects

Arrow   The grass near bamboo or hail
               Round leaves, flat boats on
smoke   a river of violet oats, foam
               In water, the tangerine color dispersed

the   In bamboo
               hail and colts
important   the circulation of boats
               the violent association
city   Tangerine absent-minded
               The official held in low esteem

Distracted
in Mandarin green

The absent reeds
The Mandarin green screw
of the pear tree
Smooth boats hulled in round leaves
a river of violet oats
watermoss, the lawn is extinguished

The vital city with bamboo and hail
river of moss, water
scatter the green

The official held in low esteem
The grass dispersed to green and exhausted
scattered the green screw of the pear tree

44. Things that Cannot be Compared

That   Harm and day
tree: Laughter and its anger
              A small blue factory and a large philodendron
faintness   When the love somebody was, stopped
              It is estimated that he became somebody different
and   In a garden completely
              the crows are in sleep
paper   Their faintness deviates from other trees

Garden   And day damaged the sun
              When the love someone has been, interrupted
              It is estimated that someone from different
and   even if it is always the same person
              A garden house to be complete: crow asleep
              Time towards the house
birds: Crow within an unexpected tree
              Wide awake, a great wind squall
the   and begin to elicit the approximate
same   Faintness turned aside with other trees
love   Cawing in the warning

              A garden marries a crow

still   Then toward the center of the night
              crows wake up and flutter approximately
stops   Their restlessness spreads to the trees
suddenly As different as the same crows in the time called "day"

              The garden entirely of evergreens
              and the center of night
              an excitement to vibrate approximately

Too   If it is too still to stop loving someone
      Everyone the same person created
still   If a garden of trees, then crows sleep completely
      When it stops in the center of night
to stop   restlessness separates other trees

      and soon birds were startled by their own dream

57. SPLENDID THINGS

A: In the room where originates the letter "S"
            Element clear it does not
purple anything and applies
That which blooms, whether thread or paper
But between the purple flowers and I
in spite of the luxurious night, I do not like the iris
When night is obligation, design occurs in snow

B: The knife decorates Chinese brocade
            The Buddhist grain of the eastern coat tree
Wisteria colors it beautifully
in the place of circumferences
Five days lay east of the pine tree
the flowering basin which knits
an Empress into the source room
The gun colored material
The thread is paper
It hangs color
The ingredient space, which it provides bloom that
But the luxury inside military discipline
between the color of the flower and I
The iris inside malice to dry
There is a silence which a trillionth
of night does not understand
Panting the colors of the 6th Chamberlain
the eye is complete

C: Grains of Buddhist thought decorate the knife
            Inside the eastern sky, wisteria blossoms
inside the pine tree
The water in the basin weaves, originates the Empress' room
A gun-dyed material
Thread and paper hand color unto any person
combined with that ingredient space

While military discipline frequently
does not like the iris
its malice dries in the night's silent trillionth
The design and when charm is quite

D: A Chinese gibe will decorate the sword
          The coat of many parts
When starting is paper
and frequently stops the color of any person
The interior luxuriously soldiers
whom the discipline frequently does not love
Inside, the iris in him drying in spite
has the quiet trillion made the night

E: Chinese mockery and calibration
          The knife supplies itself
The wisteria waves in the pine tree
Discharge the space that was the Empress
The rifle colored her as hardware
She disappeared
Paper frequently stops color
Doesn't she love within him a screen?
Calmly trillionth to form night

F: Color unloads the Empress
          She does not form love inside the screen
Design enchantment out of
colors officially seen

G: The flowering wisteria
          longs for color in a beautiful way
meshes around the pine wood
Empress?
The room of origin and picking the grape of an "S"
The glade that ago applied the element blooms
If the thread, then the paper

H: The flourishing ramification
       that is wisteria
colors wonderfully around the length
points toward pine wood
If the spinal cord, then he is paper
I in resentment in luxurious
cannot taste design or enchantment

I: The blade and envelope
       decorate Chinese damask
Where is the origin of the grape?
The site where elements bloom
If the cord spirals into his paper
But between the purple flowers
I in resentment
in luxurious color
in the obligation of night
in the design of enchantment
The garden is totally covered in snow

J: The thread, the paper
       pure-polarizes each possible form
An object blooms
If the wound remains cable he is the paper
For nature, obligation at night, something
We can't design the garden covered totally in snow

K: Ramification blossoming
       Wisteria that colors wonderfully
The size around makes a point
Empress in place of origin
Opened, that he makes purple to all things
and that is applied
But luxury enters the flower
of I in resentment
and I do not taste my own diaphragm
My obligation is to inhabit the night

design something that enchants
make a garden covered in snow

L: The Chinese language is covered with brocade
           A colored helix the size of around
making things seem artificially wisteria-ed
The Empress of beginning

M: If the spiral shellfish aligned
           To be all things, if things being opened
I exactly in the resentment of luxurious color
The obligation which is night
makes an extraordinary design and it fascinates
It is the total sum of the garden and the snow

N: The gun moral initialed place
           The bare electric wire, older brothers, crustaceans
It exiles
I not being exact participates
The silence in which the letter "D"
exists as a medical design
We manufacture and pant
the sensual pleasures inside the night
In the taste inside military discipline
indignation is not accurate

61. One of Her Majesty's Wet Nurses

The Empress wrote the following sentence: "When you go east,
illuminate the magenta in the manuscript of the sun, the unlimited rain
within this city. Look."

A portable message

East elucidates magenta in the sun
this volatile view of the city

   He was a captain in the domicile of ideas

   "If it clears in the east, very much magenta the sun"

   A captain in the domicile of Gone

In the hardware, the carcass of the traveler

A lateral consideration of the scene:
the space free above the east
the sky collates under limitless rain

I do not know this type of housewife
her stations of distant work

The lefthanded side of day
Because the final gift:
the traveller's animal corpse
The stormy city, the many-rained capital picture

   The left hand is sympathetic today
   The writing absorbs water
   The house of reduction
   It is an Empress, a storm in the place that cries
   The picture which is unimportant is this city

     and it has placed you outside consideration
     Inside the writing, the Empress

The nation revises
itself in limitless rain:
the city

Link hands sympathetic in protection
The writing does not suck on water
The figure, which is not the city
is outside lateral consideration, sameness
In the lower part of writing
boundless rains and a temporary target
which leave in her writing the possible him

The nurse absorbs
the captain in the domicile of Goes
The space is free above the east
very very magenta with sun
The sky collates under limitless rains

     Today lefthanded
     she is proofread under limitless rain
     Empress: the storm
     The picture which in unimportant
     is this city
     Inside the writing, lies the Empress
     Her nation revises the sun

Link hand sympathetic
today's day protects health
If this consideration of sameness
is extreme, then the sun
The lower regions of writing
the boundless rains
the temporary target of the city

Too much wind renders this animal inoperative
Her figure travels the hardware of bodies
The usual inward of writing
and the taking on of the persona
who leads more to rubber and paganism
Slide back transversal daily
The housewife spills a glass of blood
It is "is"

        The hand which inserts the day
        accommodates this and decreases that
        Writing for the sake of another
        that does not inhale, that shouts
        The sun's acquisition should remove
        The back section of the daily news
        is known to comprise the housewife's blood
        The housewife, the I which is not spilling
        Possible the message left in writing:
        a mobility that is revision

76. During the Long Rains in the Fifth Month

There is something very mobile
about a place with a pond
Looking in concentration
at the sky opacified
Not only in winter
when she likes to lie awake
and note that water has more cold in it
Wild and covered in bad grasses
I find moonlight very constant

> Between the rain, May is too long
> The water's dense iris
> And all gardens being
> the same green color seem that way
> There is movement in the sky
> opacified
> Liking the fact that I've become aware
> of the cold year
> Attention to a certain thing in the water

As for the pond
everything which is not better is carefully shown
The bad grass where I was covered in wildness
The necessary night is thin
I, a portable type, find moonlight in every lake

The ponds which I like
are those in which everything is carefully represented
I prefer much that is wild
in false grasses
in the portable moonlight

> A lagoon
> between two screens

I move morning into salt
into her crowded iris

During the long rain
between right and wrong:
a lake of green water
Entire the day, and the sky opaque
The taste of I is not enough
The palace of cure is representative
I appreciate extremely
that wild gram
the irises piled up
The night cannot observe moonlight
even when moonlight enters extremely

        Inside the fifth month
        a period of long rain gives crab to silence
        When time is incorrect with green scandal
        the furniture, inside out, reverses
        One green military discipline inside a child
        The sky is opaque, it sees!
        The poem widens between kicks
        Swallow the angle of the year and it wakes
        for the green branch scandal

Between the needle and the lake

Her pen diminishes the road
which is written inside winter
The night, your park, is frequent
Observe the moonlight inside water
Day, when it is possible, enters
in order to discover its own reversal

        The long rains clamp onto silence
        onto the false green scandal written in furniture
        The sky is impermeable, broad

The green branch scandal written into winter
The screen accumulates the process

The fifth month gives crab to his silence
The green scandal, the reverse of the lake
The fact that movement is distant
this sky opaque, poetry between kick and normality
Swallow the angles of the year
where it is wild and interior, her iris

During May, the crab of silence is sometimes him
When inside the box, scandal is inaccurate
I, giving, and the green waters observe the furniture
Between the screens, you ask that green be sufficient
The lake: a scandal of poetry
a flexible pried branch of a green thing
Kicking is normal for an angular year
The edge is understood excessively
The process of representation: zone and palace
Everything is appraised:
wildness and the iris ticket
Time removes the mountain elaborately

During May, we silence the crab with some time
when the scandal is not precise
The I gives differently
drapes the furniture with green and observation
The width of poetry may distinguish time
makes the discovery, the angle of revision
waters the green and nimble dyeing green branch scandal
tastes like the lake
To process portrayal and place
I arrive extremely
with a wild ticket iris

During May, an average long time
the quiet crab hour

when scandal is inexact
Observation briefly stops in the lake
You come to solicit undulation
green agile water
to dye green the ramifications of scandal
All being to consider, I arrive and have an end
to be wild, take your tickets
This mountain, possible matter
Day invests in the reversal of a clear moon

80. Things That Have Lost Their Power

In order to melt a woman
a large wooden wind
has at its root, air
The woman as him has gotten angry
The trifling husband goes from the house
and hides somewhere
convinced of the fact that
an indifference to rage is shown
meaning that she cannot be permanently restricted

        With the spring tide in decline
        the boat is high in his admission
        Melt the hair of a woman
        Nobody old in addition to being thin
        Owing to the fact that indifference to fury is shown
        its significance cannot be limited in a permanent way
        Pride turns over

Nobody always except besides it being thin
The fact is anger, indifferently demonstrated
A sense of pride or reassignment

Drying out from its holidays, the boat rests
The violent storm outside the wooden side
Some importances condemn support
Nobody always, excluded except is
She hurries over him in search of order
This fact indifferently is demonstrated as annoyance
A durable way of meaning
It is not possible to understand enclosure or pride

        The relative festivities
        in the short fuse of a woman
        It effects you, the violent storm outside your wooden side

The outline is demolished
The woman is caught up in it annoyingly
in the married surplus of a man

The relative vacation of their house
The hidden parts of approximatea
She hurries over he in search of order
They have convinced the facts indifferently
Relative to limit, the durable meaning of sense
The relative sense of pride
The renewed allocation is not possible

The boat dries in its holidays
In the end, to melt the woman with short hair
the diagram of her is demolished
Some importances condemn sustenance

The married excess of a man is shaped like a question
The hidden parcel of approximatea
She hurries on her orderly search
It is not possible to understand this wall

The hair, in short, in order to melt passing all
The man marries the trifling question
She is urgent once outside meaning

Anger marries this house
The room contains pride as a direction
She is urgent but will put it smooth
They are indifferently disturbed

Seclusion competes and demolishes
criticisms and importance
He enters the periphery under her
Marry this house and holidays will be approximate
She is pressed inside and smooth
Her research of him, an interior significance
The part of pride that replaces the self's characteristics

Efficiency inside has a vibration
that competes with seclusion
That this man vexedly let this woman arrive
to approximate the holidays in skin

> You who have become skillful at storms
> The marriage contains the skin of things
> their clay remains
> Investigation of indifference obstructed

To understand how these sheetrocked walls approximate pride
and the relative festivities found in skin

84. I Remember a Clear Morning

A: The dew was motionless
           On the barriers in bamboo and the hedges
across criss scraps of cobwebs where the startings were broken
The drops of rain stopped on them
like character strings of white pearls enchanted

While is became sunnier, the dew gradually disappeared
the clover and the other factories
The branches started to stir, suddenly by their own agreement

Later I described to people how vain it all was

B: I remember a morning-free day when it rained completely
           Despite lighting up, the sun that was rope dropping
took the form of chrysanthemums in the garden motionless
In the hedges over criss I saw scraps of iron
and the rain stopped on them like
character strings of white beads interrupted
I shifted and the branches began to agitate themselves
suddenly from their own declaration or agreement

Later I described for people how futile

C: I am the memory of a morning-free day
           And on the barriers over the criss I have seen refuse, iron
I have refused the networks of the spider
As a series of characters, the interrupted white men were
While they have become fuller than the sun
fuller than the one that disappeared fields and factories
they have been many forts in agreement

D: Despite the system lighting up the sun
           the rope drops and the sun renders the chrysanthemum motionless
In the bamboo barriers, I was chained to refusal

and a series of characters
To become fuller than the sun
and to disappear gradually the rope and other plants

E: Remember when it rained all night
          despite the bright sun
and the calm fat chrysanthemums in the garden
On the bamboo fence, rain drops were interrupted
The clover and other operations disappeared gradually
The branches caught you, touch you suddenly from their own drive
Later I described to you how beautiful everything was he

F: In spite of the luminous sun
          the rope was fat and calm
The operation to be spar, gradual

G: For the report, there was a free morning in the ninth month
          when it rained all night
The luminous sun twists in grease calms
roasted those chrysanthemums in the garden
On the bamboo fence, spider fabric
Add to that, a gradient white

This cord, that narrow field in situ
This developed without informing their clean reader

Later on I described how much beauty it cost

H: Despite lighting up, the sun torsioned in fat to calm
          and then the rain began to fall
to which add white characters upward gradient

The main cable, the narrow luzerne and variation

I: To weigh the value of illumination: the sun
          Calm fat, torsion down
A man moving toward a hill

This main alloy, luzerne and variation
to tighten in type for progression
Go and support clean reading, and see how much beauty it costs

101. Squalid Things

An evening gown with fur sticking out from the seams
Darkness which does not give the impression of being clean
She embroiders the inside of a cat's ear
This fur, that evening dress not sutured to borders
This slight defect tumbles out:
She is not especially devoted to him

This fur which impersonates the cloth of evening
On the other hand, charm
Most love appears on him
The fur always from the revolution of the nest
the cloth of nighttime, those unlined edges
On the other hand, charm is not in love with the child
Madame has the defect of falling

Purity is performed quite and because
The impression widely known as darkness
becomes very clean
Charm and its cultivation big inside her
This fault, unwell, comes to tremble

Of this skin sewn as cloth or nighttime
This blackout known extensively as place
Through embroidery, an interior enchantment of the hand
Who is not interior to this and to love?
Imperfection trembles
He comes to shake the shutdowns
that the Madame has kept together
He is special
Under monopolizing he separates from her
because love is the greatest ignition of the internal song

You go out of your way to embroider a cat's ear
The skin always a social stratum, the nighttime's cotton

inside skin
Outside this enchantment of the hand
a huge interior which loves
He separates under the monopoly of her

She leaves manners embroidered into time
Time, the night inside this skin
Light passes the largely unknown darkness in him
The impression of place
The most enormous love burns, her ethanol squalid

They leave stricken
Skin as always, a social repossession
The cotton material that forms time. The night uses it up
Pure marks also completely, because this light exceeds
which largely does not admit the density of the place
He reads about the abolition of the work

Night uses up time within this skin
Light exceeds this incompleteness
which largely did not admit the density
The impression of a place lit up
Because the internal song is busy
their ethanol squalid

112. When a Woman Lives Alone

She should be wasted
her mud should fall in pieces
If there is a pond
it should be invaded by factories of water

       It is not essential that the garden be covered by wise brush
       but the bad grasses should turn to sand
       This gives to the place a glance intensely sorry
       I hate a woman's house when it is clear that
       it has scurried approximately
       A glance without knowing which face it came from

The puttied wall should fall into the pond
It is not essential that the garden be quilted in wise brush
bad grass showing the intelligence of sand
The view arranges her face
The gate closed, as if at the end of verse

       Cement an extreme form of wastefulness
       She is an expression of her house
       The pond, its own water factory
       The garden which wears the kilt of suitable, lucid brush
       Her view becomes volatile and skillful
       as she rearranges her surfaces into a glance
       Her gates are maintained strictly

It is the abnormal game of a woman to penetrate
the falling parts of his walls
The extreme wastefulness when she expresses her house
The grass diminishes itself into sand
She skillfully reorganizes her own surfaces
"How much I would rather end the hatred for this house"

In this game, if he comes to penetrate the cement wall
he will rest in her temporary vistas
This is woman's play
if you come to penetrate her autumn walls
acts according to factories and salt water

She has adapted to brush, Scotland's skirts in this garden
He accurately undertakes direction
reorganizes her surfaces
How many I's to hate . . .
The gate rigorously adopts the cross

       Autumn's concrete expression of waste
       the bursting of this thing called "house"
       Rest. Sadness. We've reorganized her surfaces
       If you have a covering, something to accept the hating
       Mrs. Similarity! So much for limitation

If you come to see this drama
where the woman is unusual
follow her to the water factory, the seawater lake
There is a certain behavior in the destruction of wastefulness
If you come to this game
where the woman is uncommon
wasteful of intense things

       Destruction is simply one behavior
       We only have a little defective control
       here and there
       The I reconstructs its limitation
       the foundation of some You in that surface
       Something hurries her toward acceptance
       toward the water factory and his face in it

114. It is Delightful When There Has Been a Thin Fall of Snow

Coal   When snow is as thin as autumn
           we sit in an evening that revolves around braziers
           the iris chatted in dark falls
ash   We discuss various migrations
           It was as if this very evening swindled
           the night of all footsteps
           We want to know who Perhaps is
step   Middle thoughts quote the poem in her long hair

A mean autumn filled with snow
and night: an ironmonger
Several friends of similar character caused darkness to fall
When the letter "A" falls in the form of snow joy
Pull up the night covers, evening around your ears
Laughter discussed immediately as an inclination toward ash

As   Their skin increases
           at the footboard of evening
the   The person gets near, there are announcements
           "When the Empress today recognizes snow
noise   I will come quickly to meet her in the form of days"

On the veranda, a trap to measure the density of sleep
iron revolves inside evening
The kind of points that can be laughed
immediately an ash inclination is discussed
since skin noise increases
A possible we, whom we would like to know

A   Snow peels, its continuation confronts him
           piled up inside the writing they quote
different   The evening seasoned with questions, each one identically
                       chiseled
           First the density in the warships of sleep

bitter	then the sound arrested in skin increase
motion	That thing inside emergency

Snow peels and collates
The necessity of danger written on that tired slope, that wave
Skin proofread, piles of snow on the edge of the veranda
The eye reflects a dangerous necessity
Light disseminates, inclined toward light
The stations are bitter, their astringent movement toward prayer

Affable	Smiles argue for immediacy
frequent	The bedding inside emergency
must visit	Coal again, it is possible to work as we

Questions are piled up, note their compactness
subject to egg wants
The dangerous need to write
about the distribution of light
Bitter and astringent, preference and locomotion
Smiles when favors are in order

Average	When snow has been stacked like respect
	Summit and continuous skin
thought	a collated solid affluence
	He gently level and identical
and	an edge merchant on the veranda
fast	Do skin or bedclothes rhyme with night?

A possible Us in another time
The tendency of immediacy disputed by movement
Obstruction of the healthy increase in skin
She must visit notification, she adjusts mildly
that being comes exceedingly in meeting
Many times the topic of place, our things that speak
make the head deform
That is stale, our expression

The	Skin floats as snow
	An edge merchant returns of the veranda of sleep
eggs	The warship arranges, asks
	When her eyes write a pardon
inside	The shedding of blood to the point of laughter
	refuted in motion
	Identical dark bedclothes
hours	A state of emergency holds everything together

When autumn looks like an eye, is happy
Those of us who are piled up like heaps of evening
When chiseled darkness falls out of our friends
What kind of person sleeps in these surroundings?
The ramp of space, the reflection in his eyes
Various motion and evening
Sound arrests in skin increase
We peel from desire, eggshell
When she thinks he thought her up
When the point pulled out of the box is laughter
a season of goodness, already that
We peel as eggshell from want
Heavy bleeding and pleasant opinions
in the reference book of facial expressions

When	Darkness chiseled from persona
	in slept surroundings
descended	Cosmos in the preservation of laughter, compression, respect
	When night is a reconsideration of coal
into	When we think that she thought herself up, and fact
	descends into day and the head shuts
a mark	The place where her neck is a question mark

134. LETTERS ARE COMMONPLACE

Her relief when swallows pour out of his letters
although she is east of his joy
She worries him into another province

       His expression is comfortably huge
       which through any person would be smaller
       When you worry something into want

The letter arrives white against depression
Relief inserts its swallows into paper
Compare any person, his eastern part joyful
The probabilities
when she worries that remote area of him

       Excessive white exhibits in her any persona
       When language fails to leave the room
       darkness folds her into weakness

Any person with a delightfully large east
Their signs defeat the hope in medicine
The covering of each person arrives suddenly in a letter
Darkness becomes comparative in her

       All the swallows in his letters inserted into speech
       White marks the end of continue
       The gatekeeper lets her worry in
       an extremely ordered expression
       this terminal white mark
       Defeated hope seems like the life

This remote region in him and this letter
If he was attached to speech or fact
This signal, that this letter might defeat hope

He arrives suddenly, illustrative
all swallows and insertion
This person who is almost speech

135. SHRINES

Furu   The shrine crowned cryptomeria
                  It is interesting that this tree should
                  be a character of virtue
Ikuta   No mummy earns this confidence
                  which people insert into him
                  That Tsurayuki assembled a horse
                  when it defect was taken
Hanafuchi   and admitted as the anger of a god
                  Then it was a poetry with which god
Mikuri   treated this horse. Prayer as event

                  Furu, Ikuta, Hanafuchi and Mikuri
                  It would cryptomeria in crowned shrine
                  When a tree is virtue
                  He was each prayer answered by god
                  It was later that the shrine assembled a horse
                  A god dedicated to the poetry above

a pleasure   The wood expresses a sign of virtue
                  As for the diety of the Kyoto people
to know   who are not worthy of reliance
                  As for me, all this praying
                  with god glibly, a shrine which is answered
that   That horse of a different/thing is taking in sickness
                  for getting angry at the god thing
                  The horse heals a god and then lifts up a poem
                  a high, pleasant incident

New star enshrined
in Cryptomeria
Being this tree, expressing a fun
that indicates virtue

	For with the thing entirely: shoes
God	And answer back the enemy in me
	It intends a leisure shrine
glibly	Beneath enjoying that you hold a fact
	is a place a fact?
	}deity{ of Aridoshi
	The thing it will wear, it got angry
the	which goes into him: the time under language
shrine	That horse in the shoes, that time
	that horse in the place which heals him
	It comforts the hour: the field
	Sleep is passing that shrine
	The Tsurayuki other it was: the thing
	For the thing together is a divination sign, an event

A	Furu, Ikuta, Hanafuchi and }Mikuri{ Nova one} shrine{
	This tree is an expression of pleasure
new	To trust a person for the Kyoto god
star	The matter inside value which together does not
	have the Mama place
	For this matter together: this shoe, an answer, the enemy
	in me
	Does he care at the leisure shrine?
	He enjoys that you hold this fact
	in the place if fact
To	Matter to carry, obtain annoyance, obtain a bottle above
	making
trust	The time that is determined by language
an indication	Horse time to cure its comfortable sound
	This horse in place to sleep
of virtue	Divination to symbolize and event

New facts:
cryptomeria for pleasure
a printout of a tree
Honest displays and confidences
Shoes and their response: the enemy in me, quietly

which surround a shrine of free time
We estimate this fact

"Saint Shrine" this wood expresses
and begins a sign of virtue
It is interesting to be
As far as the deity of Kyoto
people are not worth this Mama confidence
As for me, the entire prayer with god glibly
The disease in order to obtain angry
The thing that is Tsurayuki
guided a horse, passed a shrine
God raises the poem, an event on pleasant

The confidence inside the breast inside he
Until language, the east's whole prayer with god went easily
Let's look at the god he raised inside the poem
and the event is pleasant

136. Things That Fall from the Sky

A roof from bark, from cypress
also freezing on a roof or in a garden
But if she is mixed with pure white snow
It announces all branches between clay bricks
I don't taste enamel
The snow seems surprising

I will have joined the pure snow
If it breaks down or if small: it
Everything only fell
In the way the snow which can be begun
Which is black
There is soap or drizzle or hail

Nontaste and enamel
I am the year old for the benevolent one much
In the way that snow has a power to begin
To announce a ramification between clay
More attractive
Brick marl pure target man
I to have soap it drizzles and hail

A.M. stops under degree in one roof tile
Snow to resemble or astound
To fall into a roof crust cypress
Marking time with analyzing or so small
For only falling

In the way which snow accentuates the starting
The morning stops beneath the roof

I freeze in the garden

137. CLOUDS

A: Crimsons and blacks
        When they are controlled by air
It charms downward
To see a thin wisp of cloud
Pierce a luminous moon
Colors which leave at dawn

B: Love and purple clouds, black whites
        I love the black clouds viola
To fascinate from within
The tonalities that they leave as dawn
The white clouds of rain directed by wind
The twilight of clouds gradually in order

C: I love the black viola of the clouds
        And men and the white clouds
referred by wind
Fascinate for the lower surface of the level inside inward
The faith which is described by Chinese poetry
consulted by the wind

D: Master the black viola of the clouds and the men and white
        clouds of rain
        It fascinates more for the surface under possible
When faith is the curtain that covers the dawn

E: Control the black crimson of viola
        clouds and the clouds of man
The whites of the rain
It fascinates more for surface under possible
that which considers the progressive twilight described as "cloud"
the end to which gives return
Faith, as described in Chinese poetry
as something which indicates the curtain

To consider the wisps that cover the moon
which resemble Chinese peonies

F: If you control the black high-red
            from the viola of the clouds
winds are advised
It fascinates more for the surface
the progressive twilight of faith
The moon which resembles much

G.   If managed high-red from
            the black viola of the clouds
a man in the rain recommends the wind
It fascinates more for surface
Under the possible level for the inner part of the inside
which the progressive shadow of the cloud has considered
the extremity that is faith
which is described in Chinese Poetry as something one
"stretches, visualizes, then it leaves them in the shovel"
Her extremities are considerd slivers of the moon

H.   He will be assured to recommend the high-red
            the black color of viola, the clouds that are man
The wind fascinates the surface
The gradual penumbra of consider
The wisps of the moon are similar to faith

140. Towards the End of the Eighth Month

The ears of rice were arranged as a poem
Busy, now autumn, stolen
The red inside luminous
These farmers, those glances have summer's strangest
Along August's long broken edge

Long   The United States grows, a form of rice
endings   and it harvests the person he should occupy
                Bent in order to use his hands, to grasp the green root
                        of Gone
                A bright red to gather a factory of evening into us
in Uzemasa   A barn glanced along these farmers
                Tighten and scorched, the United States
busy   which now grows itself. We stare

Unpeel the morning hours in pilgrimage
The autumn harvest starts to thin
Recently the United States was a vast quantity
aluminum, thin roots
The red which dawns up from inside the ear
This map aims to ring our flesh

The 11th   He is impressive and completely internal
                 occupying intensity with means
beginning   He is bitter, complete, like an old poem
                 Decisions rearrange the words again
                 The United States unpeels from its own establishment
recently   already in mourning and adoration

The autumn harvest begins to thin, a forced peel
Is it possible to manage justice with real duration
The types of comfort in this country?
A farmer in summertime maintaining a strange side of the map
the volatile opinion of the flesh

A	He occupies intense meaning in her
	You are saffron sent abroad
handhold	Their this he, lily they reel
	They are all in my mouth
	bitter, astringent, complete
	The poet decides the words' arrangement
tightens	Again

The autumn hour stuck between mourning and worship
The strength of this domain recently became thin
In each worker, each deadline, is an idea no longer flesh
Red and green reach through a dog
toward summertime

Red parts	They farm your intense significance
	This the trace strikes flesh from point of view
	The methods are saffron
mark	the iris reeled from his mouth
	bitter, astringent
It brings	Already the autumn hour begins in a fine, explosive powder
this country	The domain of worship, aluminum

Iris, they reel
those who are close to my mouth
A situation hits another eye and is a form of agitation
That morning was colored with aluminum, it's hours autumned
An enormous amount of worship
A morning made of red rooms
A summertime made more strange
The temporary landscape of meat and blood, the farm

It will	The methods used to harvest safflower, saffron
	This persona, this iris, reels in the months
internal	Some poet solves the arrangement of time against text
insurgent	struck against a new eye
	The adjacent discipline of the will

Almost   The autumn of this hour, this start, this precise substance
stopped   Summertime strikes temporarily as meat, in sight and

                red lacquer

147. Features That I Particularly Like

Surface differs from imageand the thrill differs from joy
Feature me someone
A glance when the screen is beautiful
Not good oak purpose
A pot or a fan with joy

A feature and the thing together in me
Who? The surface being incorrect from image
The I is frequent
I go out and empty time
I see the excess in him and it ends me
Regarding the actual beautiful surface
there is silence, the perhaps
But the good oak objective is joy
which is the possibility of seeing
When applying the surface, this thing I vigor
But from here, there is no atlas

For one characteristic but and this matter
together in me?
Fact continues to reel in joyful assemblage
The excessive quality of him finished me
Silence in the glossy hall, the place of cutting
From there, we do not name the ugly surface

Particularly in the surface: a false fig
This person and I are frequent
Continue fact, elasticity, volatile
It terminates me
with silence over the lucky, smooth hall
Only the good training aim of the oak
From there is does not, alas, amen

Particularly in fig, false surface
Elasticity the glad adhesive, tape reel, sum
Obstinate temporary sight
He becomes vivid, and he finishes me
The I full assuredly
There are no sections of Amen here

        Possibility to be delightful
        Continuation of the bottle
        which is perhaps rolled out this window
        The scurvy surface the section Amen over

If in me simultaneously the color of the materials
then a thing inside the number
The fortune of adhesion
continues the elasticity of fact
When the occurrence is extreme
there are no hours, or writing
We are all inside addition
The work which leaves a gun
in the place of me
After I is perfection
The silence of the materials when fortune is good
The intelligence to be joyful
The exit from a royal tomb is sincerity, writing

Leave behind a gun
because I germinate the work
The color of electricity and matter
The latter I are perfect in it
When ugly applies its amen, matter falls

        Frequency false
        Fortune's adhesion is strength
        Everyone sets out for silence in the materials
        And the good target rolls
        Amen the profile there the surface
        It falls together like amens

150. On About the Twentieth of the Second Month

I   Because the same Chinese jacket was still hooked

met   to her body, she did not change her clothes

But she, the dazzlingly, was beautiful

She: five layered: damask, grapes, clear gauze, blueprint, elephant eye

before   To the body under that

I felt unable to compare with the beauty

in her   of these colors, the world

Because the identical Chinese jacket attaches
Yet the main body inside her, 10,001 things the I
She the dazzle was beautiful, but the place where it spreads out
was tin. Outside the thing is triumph, the deep red Chinese lobe
On the gun-moral side of Chinese damask, there is clarity
The thread of gauze, which the lower body furnishes
A blueprint of a white environment
This army flag of the world is beautiful
and inside I felt ability

Disseminate the tin
Is exteriority a matter of victory?
Inside Chinese brocade: gun morals
Elephant eye silk attaches to skirt etiquette
in the lower body
Compare me to the world, an army flag

Because   Dark Chinese red, green

Unlined silk

the same   In the lateral Chinese rifle moralmoral rifle:

Chinese   this is obvious, this type of webart

Blueprint of a white climate

jacket   I am inside, am the ability

Since the same Chinese jacket
will surround my interiors
I in the principal body am him
Can you buy external victory in a box?
Recovery without silk, five colors traverse
A sign, an inscription of an army
can compare admirably with my interior capacities

I have not changed clothes
and always carry the same Chinese jacket
with the same dazzle
One would never see an evening gown
Chinese red, like this
Underneath, a gown of green damask:
a Chinese willow
Five layers without silk, colored with grapes
A gauze evening gown sketches my development
above an ordinary white zone
A skirt of ceremonial elephant eye
I estimated that nothing in the world
could compete with the beauty of these colors.

Together	I have modified to these dresses, the aligned ones
	Since I saw them, I must collate
morning	and always wear the same covering: pretty lustrum
I see	They never saw aligned this Chinese red color at night
	Under him, one divides
your	Chinese to night grass, ChineseChinese grass
	Five aligned nights castrate: a silk forage
branch	A cluster of grapes, a Chinese night heron

As for that, he did not modify
those which are arranged in a straight line
The edge should classify
You take so kindly to the Chinese language
but that was clean luster
Without doing, the Chinese red

is arranged in a straight line
Those that never looked use the methods of night
He who takes the straight line
in order to divide the Chinese language
encounters grass of the ChineseChinese silk
covers with grass which emasculates the straight line
outside night
Night heron, elephant eye
The straight line develops the beginning sketch of a woman
Possible the fact that you rival the world

Until now, the Chinese language has been kind
Edges are not modified inside the arranged line
But that was purity and one luster
There is kindness inside night's lines
How do the lines arrange within the Communist element?
In order to divide the Chinese language, there must be night
Silk pools over an unyielding spirit
We advance the initially rough sketch
of the woman with a straight line
Her boat opens
This military discipline is a beautiful fact
but does not complete the inside world
does not spare the possible

Two	In the morning, I type out branches
differently	classify the place that I go toward
	History was on the edge of revision
see	This coarse thread has not been arranged
	Only that is the pure everywhere glory
in	Between two weathers, there is the Chinese Communist Party
sound	which rearranges the night
	This basin woman is a summary sketch
	Advancement opens but the straight line with it: the boat
	With this military discipline, this happy fact
	that your place in the morning is possible?
assuredly	The possible I competes with the world, with forgiveness

A place to disappear
I bordered on revision
Rough starting with pure glory everywhere
But didn't time see two differently?
We divide a language at night in order to rest
A comfortable silk feeding ChineseChinese
Make a point of view, your right line matters
Chinese harm and heron
Labeled elephant eye in silk
I include a white hard external spirit
I advance the boat
Happy the fact that your morning faces east
and completes before night's remission

Silk	I was arranged through rough beginnings
	Pure fame everywhere always disappears
	Between time, two sets see differently rather than fixed
according	Divide time into language, remainder silk
	Our lifespan interior, comfortable
to	Discipline Chinese damage
	for night's heron and elephant eye
	We must form a criterion in silk
	according to instructions
command	The fortunate fact that morning is possible gives form
	to decree

154. One Day the Sky, Which Until Then Had Been Quite Clear

Strings   I observed pleasure enter the barrier
                 and it provided a letter
                 tied to the pure white sheet of a book
congeal   I could see that the jointed ink was cold
under   and the dark lines became weaker
                 The columns of writing, seeing it smile
                 became more curious

                 A bound character

his   He was a character sewn
                 to the page of a book
                 The ink was extremely dark
matter   The stations of Job

He passed by the fence
Conveyed the letter that I saw as joy simultaneously
written in pure white paper and tied
As for me, the line, the quality outside has frozen dark
Become faint depending upon the edge
As she opened I snapped
Observe the fact that the nick is sensitive
The ink was dark, very
from a certain place, namely
All the more I thought curiosity could be a form of doubt
Especially, if it was written in the dark

I   I eat the joy simultaneously
                 The letter where one is written "1"
observed   was pure and writes from the inside out
pleasure   White paper which is moored
                 The peeling bay of medicine
enter   Ink in that morals are a dark place

a	The dark place omits its edge
	Inside, the normality depended on possibility
	of seeing what writing must do to me
	Because he opens one's writing
barrier	Notch division and observe the fact which is...

writes on both sides of the paper
quite early in the dark in one decisive place
The toy inside doubt
More strongly than a field
It goes out and it is presumed "Oh"
The majority which is special wrote inside the dark ink

She seized ink which was outside the color of flame
Light and the columns of writing

161. On the Twenty-Fourth of the Twelfth Month

The Empress arranged that there should be a name
and for us a temple to aim for a secret tryst
I divided a carriage with some others
Snow descended as if it were days
The morning stopped and there was a strong wind
Black cotton soil where snow had puffed up
The rooftops were completely white
ignited by a pale moon
as though they were covered with money
The icicles seemed to be deliberately hung
like the various lengths of nights
luminous and assembled

      Blind men outside the carriage, the moonlight well inside
      Eight layers of plum and clearly red
      A coat of sunk violet
      In the openings of his casings one could see
      pink and yellows scarlet within him
      He had demolished the white dazzlingly

He recited the words, "cold drilling, it drew aside as ice."

The Empress ensured that the buddha should have a name
The snow part was air-pushed
The huts of the poor were roofed by slats of the moon

      His external the blind
      Covered in eight layers of magenta-free red
      The material stood grape colored
      with a strongly described Design

Time became cold and perforated resulting in snow

The Empress drew a salary
assessed the fact that buddha would need to name us
The snow descended, hours stopped
The black cotton soil
The poor besides were burned
The moon was sick as if covered with money
The icicles seemed to hang with incredibly good manners

> A sinkful of moonlight
> One could be Mrs. and A simultaneous
> in eight layers of fuschia, red-free and red plum
> Over this he transported a coat of viola sunk
> that he has polished with one luminous streak
> Legacies of the material: firm, grape, colorful
> One could see you indent it
> The scarlet dresses like evenings under yellow

The woman slid into the back of the car in order to prevent the luminous
    moon

I divided the stars between the others
The moon on a stick burned
The Empress arranged that we nominate the buddhas
for a private game, a tryst
I shared a covered cart with falling snow
One could see a patch of black land
where the snow was casting absentee
The rooftops were completely white despite the poor
illuminated uniformly by the moon
thatched in silver
Icicles deliberate in different lengths

> She carried a coat of descended violet
> A luminous gloss
> A strongly described design
> In the openings of his residences
> one could see the notchings

and the scarlet within him
The evening gowns of magenta-ed lower parts

"The whole night likes to spend you."

A divided carriage covered in delicious movement
Snow came to the bottom of our days
One could see a piece of the black cotton soil
where the snow had missed the frame
The pale moon wore a luminous uniform
moved across the sky like completion covered in money
Icicles hung in different duration as if they were days

       At the openings of his domiciles
       one could see notch and scarlet
       He stood in such a way, one of his legs inward

The cold in order to perforate the hours
The entire night to spend leisurely if there would be similar ones
"We will suffer a surplus of destination soon."

       The snow arrived instead of days
       exquisite movement
       the hours gusting
       the roofs were completely white with women
       their icicles deliberate and hung

I could see one courtesan
covered in eight layers of magenta, red, plum
and other white dresses of the night
On this she laid a covering of violet descending
a luminous gloss
One could carve scarlet into domiciles
Dazzle the white demolished

In the end, we subvert moonlight
by sliding into the backseat of a car

On some occasions we recite the words
"the cold ends to perforate the hour"
An excess of destination soon

A covering of coming down in viola
The night's dresses cut free
The night ended in a familiar courtesan

163. Times When One Should Be on One's Guard

Not one among us had the slightest dangerous feeling
then we were filled with a fear nearby
A wave leapt the boat

>   The sea is even, calms up to us
>   probably resembles a perfectly smooth green silk sheet
>   not very deep
>   There was sufficient fear very close to us

It was a day without luck in the clouds
The sea in it calms
A young woman has a bright dangerous feeling
The song continues to sings us after the song is over
In order to see us more as a form of shatter
I could not believe the very same sea broke us
in a single moment

>   I remembered this kind of derailment
>   That day that did not contain one fortunate cloud
>   As for the sea, there was no piece of green silk which
>   became quiet
>   until it resembled deeply an excess
>   I do not travel and did not have that feeling
>   of dangerous brightly among them

Wearing our clothes, jacketed songs
The I is pulverized
The sea level rises in desire to gather us
We fear sufficiency
Th boat is indistinguishable from the jumping waves
The boat and the I, time being extraordinary
All is broken in the sea's calm
which existed before the possibility of belief

The waves reorganize into a crucible
in the excess of that surface
When we were shiningly more dangerous
When we were songs in borrowed clothes
A reputation is an imperfection
that comes into contact with a person
We fear the thing that looks remarkably like sufficiency
The calm sea is possible in order for belief

Our songs are loaded
One silk side of desire
The She is blown up in vast amounts of ocean
The squall where wildness is diligent
This You that is indistinct, that jumps
We break and the sea is possible in its calm
before the end of belief

A constant temperature in which we imagine
the ocean resembles our surfaces
Dogs in the clouds pinned above a green silk
The way women are dangerous when they group and glitter
I break up the vast amount of richness here
into pieces of desire
What we simultaneously ask for and flee from

The flexibility of Afterwords
their reputation for imperfections
their assemblage between diligent and sincere
The pleasant idea of the I as a form of derailment
The song which marks it, coppers it
The vast quantity of the word "richness"
She enters the return of him

The pliability of writing
The diligence of a standard sincerity
The temperature of a place where affluence is recommended
The dog of the thing which has an ocean as surface
The center of the green silk cloud, here

Dangerous methods in shining seasons
or those that divide
In our songs, which fill up to the roof
the song where writing designates a metallic surface
The I of the thing craving
The quantity of the person is broken
Wildness cannot quantify the ocean

    The place where floating is good
    The place where temperature repairs the facts that
        connect us
    When we are short on song
    the return of us and how writing revises us

171. ILLNESSES

When appetite is a form of loss
I am thick at her feet, separated from her charming features
Damage and humidity, pleasant and washed away
Trouble box. Illness is pulled up out of
some common understanding
To be marked surely, largely disordered, humid
Opportunity, attractively, unhang like trousers, like asters
When illness excludes everyone, its treasure is the girl
who suffers his excess, is courageous
Concern fascinates the facts

The skin box is troublesome, pale, pulled thin
It separates her from her more enchanting characteristics
She disseminates clearly from an unusual toothache, hair disordered
Damage and humidity take bets on who will win her
who will smile in her place
Bright asters, trousered, cloaked
His eye is full of anxious discovery
in fact it charms her, his looking

The box of skin around her bothers him
When a girl directly apprehends her own hair
Pleasant, resplendent, approximately mordant
The lining of her coat, an earlobe:
soft soft as some forms of chance
Her trousers shine, her coat made from asters
Especially leaves worry on it, colorless

Skin box, sour hymns
She ends here, pale, beyond this poem's hazard
Waterlilies, appetite which both come to loss
A divination, a sign, one resplendent summary
mordant in her hands, wheat
Inside her: an atlas

inside chance, inside the bandage of a flag
Softly, softly the girl in trousers, an overcoat, the asters
Met in light, inside charm
in ore, vein, room
Place worries inside fact

        The box of her skin made praise a sour song
        The lily pond is irrevocable, our appetites thin
        The danger of grasping directly and bending approximately
        A rare badness of place, the disordered becomes stale
        The damage of the thing
        The kana outline, a mordant fortune telling

The white material of the letters "A" and "P"
a flag, a bandage, the whites of her eyes
In fear, in the painbox: nobility
Simultaneous the veins, the rooms, the ore, of this semantic woman
Certain: scream
Girl true, especially, very
and these people who finish her agony
who sing her sutras and when the clearness of her being
excludes their angular method
charmingly they write her into their rooms
Fast excessive, abundant, brave considerably: this is how it starts
Low end exposed, if place is sufficient, charm worries its edge

        Completions depend upon the box of skin
        He had the quality of grease on white
        Separate from fascination, drawn aside
        The disordered danger, the damage that is her
        In the apprehension, the box of pain that is him:
        another semantic woman
        Dogs and things visited each other dangerously
        People finished in anguish, the girl
        the delay of the sutra's will
        The charm that writes, that came into her room
        astonishes: fast, excessively, abundantly
        The worried edge of her that looks like charm

The box of skin formed a sour song around the brain
Danger dilutes the morning
A possible you examines the lily pond for asters
Appetite populates everyone
If the girl, then A, furnished approximately
She separates from her own fascination
An etching agent, a character
Girl: really, particularly, very much and these people
set into the agony of sheets
She distributes herself by angular, dangerous means
The ratio of clarity to charm
The end is dangerous and puts out
When the place is gold, facts sufficient, edges ensured
She is charm found in aster regard

        The song shaped sourly by her skin
        Separate freedom from good
        Infrequent terms exceed significance
        The thing, the clue to characterize hindrance
        More charm of a girl in trousers, in asters
        in the intelligent box of his pain
        The him is complete, there is even distress in the leaves
        He distributes himself into charm

The song forms acidly around her skin
The danger extracted from morning
Illness as a separation from the charm that sketches her outline
This mineral thing of a woman, an intelligent box of pain
The sutras of her will
When for this the gold of places

        When praise makes song out of acid
        it is clear and unique what good is
        The rare badness of the place is true
        The flag links to the eye, the internal atlas
        When light is chance, another semantic woman
        The unbearable pain assigns higher, leaves out everything

delays any sutra
Vastness writes into the space that was her
her edge worried into charm

Anne Gorrick lives in West Park, NY, and is a visual artist as well as a poet. Her poems have appeared in the journals *American Letters and Commentary, Fence, Gutcult, Shearsman,* and *Sulfur* among others. Collaborating with artist Cynthia Winika, she produced a limited edition artists' book, *"Swans, the ice," she said,* through the Women's Studio Workshop in Rosendale, NY. She also curates the reading series, *Cadmium Text,* devoted to local, innovative writing.

Printed in the United States
203745BV00003B/121-156/P

9 781848 610040